101 Tips to Become a Radical Liberal

The Ultimate Guide for Woke, Progressive and Superior Individuals

By Tanner Thomas Roberts

DEFIANCE PRESS
& PUBLISHING

ISBN-13: 978-1-948035-40-8 (Paperback)
ISBN-13: ? (eBook)

Edited by Janet Musick
Cover designed by ?
Interior designed by Debbi Stocco
Illustrated by Tanner Roberts

Published by Defiance Press and Publishing, LLC

Bulk orders of this book may be obtained by contacting Defiance Press and Publishing, LLC. www.defiancepress.com.

Public Relations Dept. – Defiance Press & Publishing, LLC
281-581-9300
pr@defiancepress.com

Defiance Press & Publishing, LLC, 281-581-9300, info@defiancepress.com

This book is dedicated to my family – Dad, Mom, Tiffany, Tanya and Travis. I am blessed to have you all in my life and to have a family that always has each other's backs. A special thanks to my Dad for leading by example to help me become a better and harder-working man. And a special thanks to my mom, whose selflessness and unconditional love has touched the lives of so many. Much of my inspiration for this book came from my family's constant mockery of political correctness. God gave me the strength not to add all of those jokes to this book and ruin us all.

Table of Liberal Contents

INTRO

You are intelligent. You are liberal. Your empathy is renowned across the political stratosphere and your compassion is unwavering in the obstacles of inconvenient facts. Essentially, you are superior to everyone else. During these times of war against the vile hate of the right, we need to remain true to the virtues we set for ourselves and others. Still, everyone can use a little guidance to achieve their apex of progressivism—a sort of road map to boost yourself up onto that perch of righteousness as the masses look to you for understanding. There are everyday battles to be won out there, so we need to harness our inner outrage and focus it like a laser beam on the opposition. The tips in this book will help bring that laser into focus.

In this book, you will learn what many highfalutin' intellectuals are currently practicing today. You too can become a statist warrior and fight like hell until all have fallen under the conformity umbrella. All you have to do is follow these tips to the tee!

 Whether it is a night out, celebrating the holidays, raising children, being a college student, sustaining in the workplace, protesting, or hanging out on social media—you too can harness the power of absolute outrage.

TRIGGER WARNING: THIS BOOK IS SATIRE.

Top 20 Tips for Everyday Practice

#1 Never Be Complacent

#2 Be Tolerant but Not Too Tolerant

#3 Russia, Russia, Russia

#4 Don't Just Say It—Scream It!

#5 It's Not Your Fault; It's Society's

#6 Demand What Others Have

#7 Only Use Religion When It Benefits Your Talking Points

#8 Misleading Facts Are Your Friend

#9 Dress the Part

#10 Change the Language

#11 Be Offended

#12 Change History

#13 Tax 'em

#14 Own the Culture

#15 Become a Character Assassin

#16 Escalate to a State of Frenzy

#17 Predicate Every Statement with "If True..."

#18 Believe All; Believe Everything

#19 Instill Guilt

#20 Create False Enemies

TIPS FOR EVERYDAY PRACTICE

#1 Never be Complacent.

A key to being a good liberal is never being happy with anything. Everything is racist, anything is sexist, and everyone is bigoted. Getting upset over the smallest details of everyday life are some of the biggest achievements. Keep hyper-aware of systemic issues that threaten our intersectionality which, thankfully, happens to be anything. Now, go out there, stay vigilant, and find something to complain about.

TIPS FOR EVERYDAY PRACTICE

#2 Be Tolerant but Not Too Tolerant.

As a liberal, you need to pride yourself on your tolerance. After all, there is no one who exudes more integrity and acceptance than your progressive self. Always be tolerant except when it comes to intolerance. The barriers of intolerance seek to block out any forward-thinking solutions that you hold true. Those thoughts, those solutions should hold true with everyone. Do not tolerate intolerance. You are way too tolerant to tolerate any intolerance from feeble-minded conservatives.

TIPS FOR EVERYDAY PRACTICE

#3 Russia, Russia, Russia...

Did a senator, congressman or, even worse, presidential candidate of the Democratic Party lose an election to a Republican? This is probably because of Russia. However, if you find yourself lacking proof of this accusation, remember that perception is everything. Repeatedly blame Russia and enough people will buy your claim, which will help discredit those Republican victories.

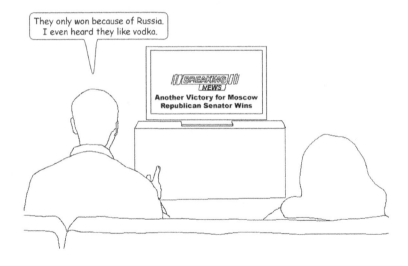

TIPS FOR EVERYDAY PRACTICE

#4 Don't Just Say It—Scream It!

Screaming not only helps get your point across, but it prevents you from hearing anyone else's opinion. But that does not matter because you are liberal and your opinion is the only one that matters. Being hysterical means being successful.

TIPS FOR EVERYDAY PRACTICE

#5 It's Not Your Fault. It's Society's.

Unhappy, overweight, unemployed, divorced, single, broke, angry, bitter—whatever it is, it isn't your fault. Society has put you at a disadvantage and treated you unfairly. The good news is everything and everyone is to blame but yourself. Reinforce that blame on society and demand that it change, not you.

TIPS FOR EVERYDAY PRACTICE

#6 Demand What Others Have.

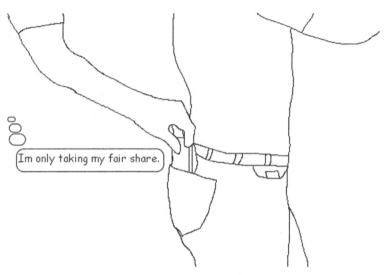

Successful people only serve as the discomforting reminder of how unsuccessful we are. Government can help make you prosperous, but first they need to take from those who have overindulged. If you personally cannot take what others have, then advocate that the government should take more. After all, it is only fair. Being a good liberal means always going after that which you are envious of. Never stop the fight and never stop demanding.

TIPS FOR EVERYDAY PRACTICE

#7 Only Use Religion When It Benefits Your Talking Points.

You may not know the difference between an orthodox Jew and a Catholic priest, but you sure know how God judges people. When you are not making fun of people for believing in some fairytale book that is used to make up their moral foundation, you can be using those same teachings against them. Don't fret. for even if you do not believe in any kind of religion, you can act like you know what you're talking about.

I am an atheist, but the Pope agrees with me on open borders. Jesus would obviously hate you.

TIPS FOR EVERYDAY PRACTICE

#8 Misleading Facts are Your Friend.

Sometimes the facts do not always work in your favor. Yet, a good liberal knows how to skew unfavorable information. Casually omitting data points can go a long way. Also, the reverse can work just as well when using broad amounts of unrelated data to make a singular, even sometimes irrelevant, point. If you find yourself losing the debate through facts, you can always name-call to distract from any sensible political discussion.

TIPS FOR EVERYDAY PRACTICE

#9 Dress the Part.

Accessorizing can help society recognize you as the trendy social justice warrior you are. If the garbs of repression are bringing you down, just use these items below to let everyone know that you are liberal and liberated.

Do not settle for the standard hair colors set by the patriarchy. Dye your hair a color (or multiple colors) to let everyone know just how edgy and progressive you are.	Tat it up randomly and often. Use tattoos that do not make sense even to you.	Remember, anything can be pierced	If you could be mistaken for a homeless person on the street, you are doing it right. Mix baggy with tight clothes and wear items that contradict the weather (a beanie in 100-degree weather).

TIPS FOR EVERYDAY PRACTICE

#10 Change the Language.

Words can change the world. We just need to take some of the hateful language out there today and make it less triggering. Emotions are our foundation and can impact the way people think about certain issues. Harness that emotion, even if it is fear-mongering or corrupt, because it will help make you appear as the better person.

Replace the phrase "minimum wage" with the words "living wage." This way anyone that supports differently basically supports a death wage.	Instead, use the words "Human American Dreamer." First off, people are humans, not aliens, and secondly, humans cannot be illegal.	The phrase reeks with toxic masculinity. Instead, let's use "Sapiens Strong" until that becomes offensive.

TIPS FOR EVERYDAY PRACTICE

#11 Be Offended.

If you follow tip #1 then being offended should come easy. This is the only way you can change the world to fit around your extremist marginal opinion. Thankfully, the world is quick to adapt to even the smallest offenses. Stay vigilant because the power of being offended could be powerful enough to ruin a funny joke, good movie, classic book, restaurant/retail store chain, a brand, a career, a reputation, history, culture, education, entertainment, etc.

TIPS FOR EVERYDAY PRACTICE

#12 Change History.

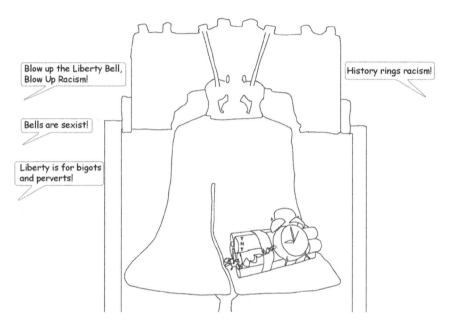

We control academics, so this should be relatively easy. However, if you are not a teacher, you can still assist in altering history. There is always a text book that needs to be rewritten or ripped up or a statue that needs to be eradicated. It is up to you and your fitful behavior to make sure this materializes sooner rather than later.

TIPS FOR EVERYDAY PRACTICE

#13 Tax 'em.

In line with #6, taxing is the most effective way to make sure those with more are punished for having too much. The only answer to how much we should tax is "more." We need to tax billionaires out of existence. We need to tax millionaires into oblivion. We need to tax hundred-thousandaires back down to earth. We need to make sure everyone pays his or her fair share except for nearly half of Americans. They do not need to pay anything.

*Extra Tip: Anyone who targets conservatives is a friend of the liberal. That friend is the IRS and we love that friend. Support the IRS any way you can.

TIPS FOR EVERYDAY PRACTICE

#14 Own the Culture.

Being a liberal has never been so easy. You get to assimilate to the same ideas found in media, Hollywood, entertainment, education, and culture. You don't ever have to come up with an original thought or idea! All of your arguments can be conjured from an actress's Twitter feed! Heck, you are on the right track in life if you think exactly like those who are super famous with millions. Then you can confirm your beliefs through one of the many news outlets, online publications, social media platforms, late-night TV shows, and movies that support your progressive agenda. Culture is yours, so bask in it.

TIPS FOR EVERYDAY PRACTICE

#15 Become a Character Assassin.

Someone making life difficult by spewing conservative hate? Are they becoming more successful and starting to have influence? No worries! Just take aim and assassinate. Dig up old tweets, writings, or high school stories that will shine a light on their deviance. Can't find anything? Well, that's okay, too, because manufacturing stories is a liberal specialty. Having the culture by your side will help spread those falsehoods and create even the tiniest amount of doubt about a person's character.

TIPS FOR EVERYDAY PRACTICE

Liberal Name Calling Dictionary

Bigots – Conservatives that are intolerant of your views.

Fascist – Pretty sure this means anyone who disagrees with the Democratic Party.

Homophobic – Conservatives that hate homosexuals, including and especially gay conservatives.

Misogynist – Conservative men that dislike women.

Patriarchs – Conservative white males that control everything.

Racist – Conservatives that hate all races except whites.

Sexist – Could mean any prejudice held against anyone of the opposite sex but really means conservative men hate women.

Xenophobe – Conservatives that hate foreigners.

TIPS FOR EVERYDAY PRACTICE

#16 Escalate to a State of Frenzy.

Take every story, rumor, or allegation and escalate it to a state of frenzy, even if you do not have all the facts first. No liberal has time to wait for the facts because we believe everyone is guilty until proven innocent. Before the facts can be released, there needs to be wide-spread hysteria throughout the news and social media. We need to rally the mob when there is any chance to assassinate the character of a conservative or others that we do not agree with. True, this sometimes leads the mob into stringing up an innocent during the process, but who cares?

TIPS FOR EVERYDAY PRACTICE

#17 Predicate Every Statement with "If True..."

The Liberal Journal
Democracy Dies in Stupidity

World News   Opion/Fact   Sports   Weather/Climate Change

BREAKING NEWS

Republican President Lies to Everyone, According to Unverified
Report. Impeachable Offense, if True.

Journalists already have this statement at their disposal for stories that make juicy headlines yet go completely unverified. Go ahead and add this to your liberal language repertoire. The glorious thing about predicating every statement with "if true" means that, no matter how ridiculous whatever precedes it, you will never be held accountable for the damage it causes if it's proven false.

TIPS FOR EVERYDAY PRACTICE

#18 Believe All, Believe Everything.

If a politician says the world is going to end in 12 years due to climate change, believe it. If an actor says he or she is a victim of a hate crime, believe it. If a prominent anchor says conservatives are all vile creatures from hell, then you better believe it. These are smart and successful people. As liberals, we all have a narrative we need to stick to and, when something fits that narrative, we have to believe it, whether it's true or not.

TIPS FOR EVERYDAY PRACTICE

#19 Instill Guilt.

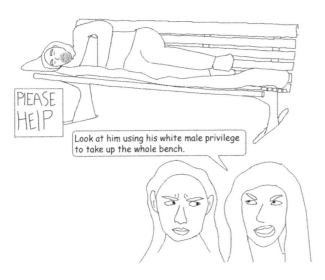

PLEASE HELP

Look at him using his white male privilege to take up the whole bench.

If they are white, they are privileged. If they are male and white, they are not only privileged, but they are oppressive. There is nothing more to it. You do not need to know someone's backstory, hardships, upbringing, or anything else that may prove that they are not exactly privileged compared to others. This general assumption may make you a miserable person, but at least you will be a woke miserable person.

*Extra Tip! Instilling guilt doesn't just apply to white people. You should make anyone who is rich feel like a terrible person for accumulating success and wealth that many Americans do not possess.

TIPS FOR EVERYDAY PRACTICE

#20 Create False Enemies.

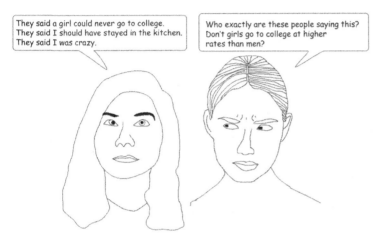

They said a girl could never go to college. They said I should have stayed in the kitchen. They said I was crazy.

Who exactly are these people saying this? Don't girls go to college at higher rates than men?

Every narrative needs an antagonist. For example, people said men couldn't compete in women's sports. Those "people" are the antagonists. Now transgender women (men but not really men) don't just compete in women's sports, they dominate them. If those "people" do not exist, you need to create them. Once they are created, you have become the protagonist. You have become the hero.

10 Tips for Obnoxious Protesting

Gear up. We are taking these tips to the streets!

#21 Burn Trash Cans

#22 Ruin People's Days and Block Traffic

#23 Destroy Private Property

#24 Chant Non-Sensical Chants

#25 Be Exclusive

#26 Make it a Payday

#27 Harass and Threaten

#28 Burn Flags

#29 Cover Your Face

#30 Start a Fight

TIPS FOR OBNOXIOUS PROTESTING

Must Have Items for Protesting

Pepper Spray
Always be prepared to spray a Nazi in the face.

Batons
Sometimes you have to beat peace into people.

Pussy Hats
Nothing says ultra-feminist like a pair of pussy ears to compliment a sassy attitude.

Lighter
Those trash cans are not going to set fire to themselves.

Signs
Signal your conformity to the world with a witty protest sign that grabs the attention of our friends in media.

Face Cover
Let's face it, we are sometimes there to just cause violence, destroy public property, and hopefully loot. If you are protesting in a liberal city (like there is any other kind of city) then chances are they won't even care you are hiding your identity from the law.

TIPS FOR OBNOXIOUS PROTESTING

#21 Burn Trash Cans.

Nothing says you are a serious protester better than setting a trash can ablaze. Impart fear into the opposition through the smell of burning plastic, cellophane, and Styrofoam. As liberals, we do not completely understand why it is necessary to burn trash cans, but we sure know it makes for one hell of a photo opportunity. Burn one and move onto the next and let the city worry about picking up the mess. After all, the city belongs to you.

TIPS FOR OBNOXIOUS PROTESTING

#22 Ruin People's Days and Block Traffic.

The optimal time to do this is around 8 a.m. during the week. This is how you catch the most attention while also avoiding responsibilities at your own job by claiming you are exercising your rights as an "activist." Sure, some fat cat capitalists are going to get irritated at you for making them a little late to their daily exploitation of their workers. Well, I say, "Bravo!" Being an obnoxious protester means being disruptive. Disrupting the flow of a system that props up the wealthy on the backs of the middle-class is a heroic undertaking, even if some of those middle-class people are included in that traffic.

TIPS FOR OBNOXIOUS PROTESTING

#23 Destroy Private Property.

Take your angry mob to the nearest business and destroy it. Double points if you can ruin the life's work of a small business owner. However, chances are there will be store fronts for large multi-chain corporations who will never condemn you for your activism. Not only can you count on the ignorance of those corporations to not condemn you, but they will probably double down on their support for your cause!

*Extra Tip! If the opportunity presents itself, loot those businesses. You worked hard to exercise your right to protest, so you deserve free crap.

TIPS FOR OBNOXIOUS PROTESTING

#24 Chant Non-Sensical Chants.

The foundation of protesting is built on the unison of gibberish chanting. Making sense is not the priority. The priority is being heard, being loud, and being involved. Messaging is important, but the sense of unity against the opposition can be more impactful than any words ever spoken. Lock arms with your brothers and sisters and let your rhetoric battle the air space that is currently occupied by the hate from the alt-righters.

TIPS FOR OBNOXIOUS PROTESTING

#25 Be Exclusive.

Be exclusive to members that only think as you do and reflect the values of your organization. This can be confusing sometimes because organizations like to claim they are inclusive and tolerant of everyone. Let it be clear that this does not apply to conservatives. We do not need hate-mongering bigots ruining our demonstrations. Remember to be exclusive when being inclusive.

TIPS FOR OBNOXIOUS PROTESTING

#26 Make it a Payday.

PAY TO THE ORDER OF ___ Little Social Justice Warrior ___ DATE ___

$1,000

One Thousand Dollars

FOR _Making Protests Seem Bigger_   *George Soros*

Free speech doesn't always have to be free. Research the many opportunities that make protesting not just gratifying, but rewarding, too. There are plenty of well-to-do activists that need your help making a rally look more successful then it probably would have ever been without some sort of compensation. Many offer travel arrangements to and from the destination of protest, leaving you with no excuse to exercise your first amendment rights.

TIPS FOR OBNOXIOUS PROTESTING

#27 Harass and Threaten.

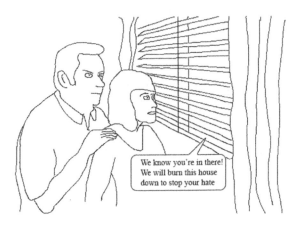

We know you're in there! We will burn this house down to stop your hate

Step 1—Target a conservative.

Step 2—Find out where the target lives.

Step 3—Surround the target's house.

Step 4—Harass target.

Step 5—Threaten the target (women and children are not excluded from threats).

Congrats, you have successfully completed tip #27 for obnoxiously protesting.

TIPS FOR OBNOXIOUS PROTESTING

#28 Burn Flags.

America has been plagued by oppression, hate, and tyranny. It deserves to burn (theoretically). Take advantage of the inordinate amount of freedoms we have in this country and burn that pennant of chauvinism we call the American flag. Don't worry; desecration of the flag is not illegal, so you are well within your rights to burn one. To add insult to injury, display the flag of another country proudly while carrying out this act, even though you have zero intentions of ever living in such a country. Resist the fear of controversy that comes along with this, as real activism is achieved through radical self-expression.

TIPS FOR OBNOXIOUS PROTESTING

#29 Cover Your Face.

If your protests include any of the more "radical" tips, then you are going to need to conceal your identity. There is nothing anyone can or will do about it. Plus, it is a bit self-gratifying to dress up as if you're going into battle. It may be a fictitious battle that pits you against a smashable store front window, but this is still a great opportunity to feel relevant. Become the social justice warrior your city doesn't deserve but needs.

TIPS FOR OBNOXIOUS PROTESTING

#30 Start a Fight.

Never start a one-on-one fight with a conservative. Those nut jobs could be carrying on the basis of some absurd "self-defense" claim. Or they might actually be able to fight back. The most effective method to take on a conservative during a protest is to outnumber him or her by at least 4-1. Add weapons to the mix and you are guaranteed to come out victorious. Do not be afraid to punch a Nazi in the face, for you will always have the backing of your fellow comrades.

10 Tips for a Progressive Night Out

It is hard to stay a diligent liberal on your nights off. But progressivism never takes a night off. We need to keep to our convictions in the real world.

#31 Choose Your Movies Carefully

#32 Avoid Culturally Appropriating Restaurants

#33 Be a Craft Beer Snob

#34 Avoid Ladies' Night

#35 Drink to No Fault

#36 Be Slutty

#37 Do Not Hit on Girls

#38 Modern Art

#39 Make World Issues a Talking Point at Every Party

#40 Do Not Let Conservatives Go Peacefully Into The Night

TIPS FOR A PROGRESSIVE NIGHT OUT

#31 Choose Your Movies Carefully.

Is the main actor a heterosexual white male? Yuck, skip that one. The more diverse the cast, the more likely the movie will be a hit. Nothing makes a project more successful than a bunch of people that look different but think the same. Are the characters authentic? For example, is the Indian character played by an Indian, is the paralyzed character played by a paraplegic, is the doctor played by a real doctor, is the 73-year-old woman played by a 73-year-old woman, is the ghost child played by a real ghost, etc. After all, movies are more than just pretend play time. They are culture-defining pieces of art that need to be taken seriously.

*Extra Tip: To act as a feminist when deciding what movie to watch, be sure the film has passed the Bechdel Test. The Bechdel Test has a very basic requirement: there must be two women that talk about something other than a man.

TIPS FOR A PROGRESSIVE NIGHT OUT

Stay in the 94%

A great guide to use when deciding on a movie to watch is the "Oscar 94." Check the list of movies that have either won an Oscar or have been nominated.

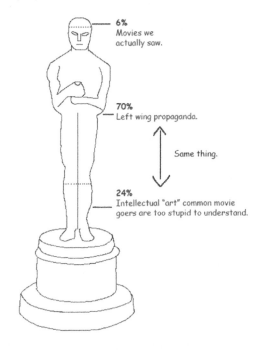

6%
Movies we
actually saw.

70%
Left wing propaganda.

Same thing.

24%
Intellectual "art" common movie
goers are too stupid to understand.

#32 Avoid Culturally Appropriating Restaurants.

Going out for Chinese? That's great, but ask yourself this question, who is running that restaurant? Is it an authentic person of Chinese descent, or is it some white-washed American version of Chinese food? Your culture palate will never be as sophisticated as you want if you eat a white man's egg roll. Be wary of America's manifest destiny of culture cuisine. Supporting these establishments means you are supporting culture appropriation, which in turn means you are a horrible racist.

TIPS FOR A PROGRESSIVE NIGHT OUT

Culture Appropriating Food: DO NOT EAT

Leave it to Americans to completely disgrace a culture and pass these dishes as "authentic." Below are merely just American inventions used to exploit other cultures for a buck. Avoid your appropriating appetite by skipping these meals:

General Tso's Chicken   German Chocolate Cake   Queso   Spaghetti and Meatballs

French Roast Coffee   English Muffins   Fortune Cookies   Chimichanga

TIPS FOR A PROGRESSIVE NIGHT OUT

#33 Become a Craft Beer Snob.

Discuss your thoughts on the need of intersectionality's influence on western culture with a cold, unheard-of beer. You have already established your intellectual superiority, now emphasize it by loudly sipping your foul-smelling ale while pretending to listen to someone else's less-relevant point. Everyone wants to hear the point of view from the person that can name 147 different IPAs off the top of their head. Be that person.

TIPS FOR A PROGRESSIVE NIGHT OUT

#34 Avoid Ladies' Night.

We are made to believe that ladies' night is designed to cater to women's needs and wants. What it is instead is another way to sexually objectify women so bars can bring in more revenue. Let's serve women cheaper drinks, get them intoxicated quicker, and have men make unsolicited passes at them. What a great plan! If your gal pals are planning to attend a ladies' night, opt out to stay at home to watch recorded Rachael Maddow episodes by yourself. Then vilify your friends later.

TIPS FOR A PROGRESSIVE NIGHT OUT

#35 Drink to No Fault.

One of the few acceptable excuses to avoid responsibility is to excessively drink and blame your actions on the fact that you were drunk. The term kids use these days to skirt accountability is "blackout." Emotional tirade? You were drunk. Threatening actions? You were drunk. Hooked up with someone you wish you hadn't? You were blackout. This is a safeguard to any regrettable action.

TIPS FOR A PROGRESSIVE NIGHT OUT

#36 Do Not Hit on Girls.

Fellas, just don't do it. You could be sued or slandered. Just don't do it.

TIPS FOR A PROGRESSIVE NIGHT OUT

#37 Be Slutty.

To be slutty is to be empowered. Nothing evokes feminism like sleeping with hundreds of random dudes. In addition, the more you sleep with, the more likely you'll get the opportunity to get an abortion. After that milestone, you will have hit the pinnacle of feminism and can now join the campaign of "shouting your abortion." You go, girl.

TIPS FOR A PROGRESSIVE NIGHT OUT

#38 Make Time for Modern Art.

Keeping cultured requires a good rotation of modern art exhibit visits on your nights out. You risk seeming a little pretentious, but a good liberal never worries about too much posturing. Your sophistication trumps any perception of those that enjoy modern art. Come equipped with words like expressive, provoking, enigmatic, perplexing, transcending, and whatever other adjectives you can find on the internet.

TIPS FOR A PROGRESSIVE NIGHT OUT

#39 Bring Controversy to the Party.

Break the norms of mundane socializing by stirring up a politically charged tirade at your next gathering. Provoke controversy while simultaneously limiting the "good times" vibe. Movies and entertainment do this all the time by inserting a political quip that alienates half the audience, which usually prompts eye-rolls from those less progressive. But this is okay because we can separate the virtuous from the vile. Make parties great again by bringing awareness to issues you believe need to be discussed over anything else that may be more joyful.

TIPS FOR A PROGRESSIVE NIGHT OUT

#40 Do Not Let Conservatives Go Peacefully into the Night.

If you are at a restaurant, in a bar, at a gas station, at a concert, at a football game, the theater or wherever else and you spot a conservative, be sure to make your presence known. Let them know they are not welcomed out in public. Harass and threaten them, even when they are with their family. This will prompt your fellow comrades to join in on the shaming. Force them out of any establishment and be sure to leave an impression that says, "You are not welcome here." Eventually, you will be able to convince said establishment to stop serving conservatives all together.

10 Tips For Fixing Holidays

Holidays are a great time to get together with the family and remind them exactly what they are commemorating. It may ruin the celebration but, as you will learn, not everything should be celebrated equally

#41 Fix Fourth of July

#42 Police Halloween Costumes

#43 Never Say "Merry Christmas"

#44 Woke New Year's Resolution

#45 Recognize White Privilege in Santa

#46 Do Not Give Thanks to Genocide

#47 Be Hyper Aware of Columbus Day

#48 Become Culturally Cognizant of Holidays

#49 Down with Nativity!

#50 Seize the Opportunity

TIPS FOR FIXING HOLIDAYS

#41 Fix Fourth of July.

Come Join Us July 5th to Celebrate the Birth of a New Nation. Reject the Celebration of Rich, Slave-Owning White Men Refusing to Pay Their Fair Share of Taxes. Come Together as We Talk About How Terrible this Country is Starting with its VeryFoundation. It Might Not Be as Fun as Actual Fourth of July but it Will be Much More Progressive!

Ask yourself, what exactly are we celebrating on the Fourth of July? The fact that a bunch of rich white men didn't want to pay taxes? That is a battle every day in this country to date. Would we ever celebrate the fact that men today try to avoid paying their fair share during times of such income inequality? One could argue that it is celebrating the birth of our nation. But nothing is commemorative over a birth of a nation with systematic racism, bigotry, inequality, male dominance, and an endless list of other discriminations.

TIPS FOR FIXING HOLIDAYS

#42 Police Halloween Costumes.

How dare you mock the mummy culture like that! Don't you know hose people are dead! No candy for bigots!

Halloween has been an excuse for cultural appropriation for generations. It is a chance for those ignorant individuals to dress up like some type of offensive cultural stereotype. To top it off, women tend to take things to another level of mockery by making that costume as slutty as possible. Cultures are not costumes meant for your enjoyment and they are especially not meant to be gawked at by some drunken guy at a party. Making the world a better place means you have to sacrifice some fun at your next Halloween revelry in order effectively police costumes. Someone has to tell that "slutty" ninja that ninjas are real people with feelings. People all over the world will thank you.

TIPS FOR FIXING HOLIDAYS

#43 Never Say Merry Christmas.

We have been working on this one for years, people. The good news is, we are winning the battle. However, we can never be complacent (remember tip #1). There are still many of us that receive Christmas cards with the words "Merry Christmas" shoved in our faces. You may celebrate Christmas in the sense that you set up a tree, you decorate your house, you buy presents, you listen to holiday music but you should never actually state the holiday you are actually celebrating.

TIPS FOR FIXING HOLIDAYS

#44 Make Progressive NYE Resolutions.

You can be a typical, self-centered individualist with your New Year's resolution by focusing on things such as trying to lose weight or spending more time with the family. Or you can awaken your mind to the virtues of progressivism. Make a resolution to be more involved in activism. Do things like avoiding right-leaning businesses, creating a racially driven hoax, watch more of Michael Moore, or making time to threaten those with different opinions on social media.

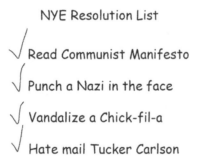

NYE Resolution List

√ Read Communist Manifesto

√ Punch a Nazi in the face

√ Vandalize a Chick-fil-a

√ Hate mail Tucker Carlson

TIPS FOR FIXING HOLIDAYS

#45 Recognize White Privilege in Santa.

Imagine someone of color breaking into your house in the middle of the night, leaving "goodies" for your kids and eating your food. This sounds like a recipe for a frantic call to 911, right? Well, because this person is white and privileged, we accept it. We need to recognize that we are making a martyr out of an abuse that has plagued our nation for centuries. Do away with Santa this holiday season and rid your holiday of white male privilege.

TIPS FOR FIXING HOLIDAYS

#46 Don't Give "Thanks" to Genocide.

Can you come in the kitchen and help me with these mashed potatoes, dear?

Screw you, Grandma, and your ancestors and your unjust holiday!

Predatory colonialism has been normalized and whitewashed into an annual celebration. Gluttonous Americans celebrate the genocide of Native people by over-indulging in subpar dishes while being forced to see relatives that they prefer to see from the distance of social media. This is known by the masses as Thanksgiving. How about we not give thanks to our homicidal ancestors for nearly killing off all indigenous people? Celebrate Black Friday all you want, but next time offer yourself to lead the blessing at the table. This will give you the opportunity to speak truth to power.

Extra Tip! Thanksgiving prayer: Dear God, we thank you for giving our ancestors the power to rid Natives of their rightful homes so we can stuff our faces hundreds of years later in celebration with people we barely even like. Amen.

TIPS FOR FIXING HOLIDAYS

#47 Be Hyper Aware of Columbus Day.

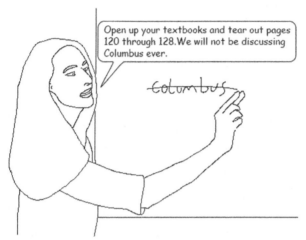

Much like Thanksgiving, Columbus Day is a yearly reminder to feel guilty about this western civilization we have been forced into. Admittedly, Columbus and his settlers may have inadvertently brought death to indigenous people through disease, but they also brought the virus of western culture that continues to infect today. The more we learn about Columbus, the more we realize how dated this holiday is becoming. Many cities have already done away with Columbus Day and have now replaced it with Indigenous People Day. Sure, some of the indigenous people were not exactly pacifists, but let's stick with that because it makes us appear more caring.

#48 Become Culturally Cognizant of Holidays.

You celebrate Christmas without actually *celebrating* Christmas. What is the difference with any other holiday? The difference is you can look more cultured by recognizing holidays that are not as mainstream as Christmas. The calendar is full of them. People will admire your intelligence and recognize you as a leader in ethnic awareness.

TIPS FOR FIXING HOLIDAYS

#49 Down with Nativity!

For once, it would be nice to celebrate the holidays without being reminded it is Christmas time. Nativity scenes on both public and private property are erected monuments made to remind us that religious discrimination is alive and thriving in this nation. There are atheists that celebrate the holidays and they prefer not to be force-fed religious nonsense during this time. We need to consider other people's beliefs (or lack of) while reconsidering the beliefs of Jesus.

TIPS FOR FIXING HOLIDAYS

#50 Seize the Opportunity.

The fact is you cannot always avoid these holidays. Chances are you are going to be suckered into a family gathering that forces you to actually talk to your relatives. Might as well use this opportunity and pull out that soap box. People need reminders of how ignorant and uneducated they are. Who better to do that than the perfect refined liberal of the family? Skip the talks of your cousin's newborn. Instead, educate that cousin on why her little natural resource-sucking bundle of cells is going to aid climate change and the destruction of our planet.

10 Tips for Raising Children

Having kids presents a great opportunity to guarantee that a progressive agenda will be passed down for generations to come. These are some great tips to prevent your child from being a little capitalist fascist piggy.

#51 Do Not Assign a Gender

#52 It Takes a Village

#53 Minimal Discipline

#54 Accept Dependency

#55 All Children are Winners

#56 Associate with the Opposite

#57 Mothers, Lock Your Sons Away

#58 Let Them Vote

#59 Exploring Sexuality

#60 Keep Them Publicly Educated

TIPS FOR RAISING CHILDREN

#51 Do Not Assign Gender

The obvious signs of gender can be observed right at birth. However, this is only a biological scientific fact, not a socially acceptable fact. Your baby has not decided what it wants to be yet. Do not make life harder for it by assigning a gender that it may want to change later down the road. Instead, give it no gender or identity.

TIPS FOR RAISING CHILDREN

#52 It Takes a Village.

Responsibility of parenting is not just on the parents. It's on the village. It's on the community, the government, and sometimes other people's time, effort, and money. Children do not just belong to their parents or families. They belong to the whole community. They need to be programmed safely into the perfect society we are trying to create. Your children belong to us. The family unit has failed at raising tolerant children.

TIPS FOR RAISING CHILDREN

#53 Use Minimal Discipline.

Neglect spanking. If you are still using the archaic disciplinary method of swatting your child's behind, you might as well report your repugnant self into CPS. Other methods of negative reinforcement, though less violent, are just as ineffective as spanking. Instead, children need to be treated with care, dignity, and taught they are unique, just like every other child. Disciplining just creates resentment.

TIPS FOR RAISING CHILDREN

#54 Accept Dependency.

Your children depend on you for love, care, support, and nurturing. Age never changes that. In fact, the older they get, the more support they may need. The world is a ruthless place and it is your job to nurture them through it. So, if your 28-year-old son is not ready to move out of the house and become financially independent, it is your duty to accept that dependency. Kids need security and you can help them feel secure while requiring minimal effort from them.

TIPS FOR RAISING CHILDREN

#55 All Children Are Winners.

Children do not come in second, let alone last, in anything. How are we supposed to instill inclusion and fairness on our kids if we give all the spoils to the victor? One way is to ensure that, whatever recreational sporting activity we place them in, does not define winners and losers. A world where there is no downtrodding of losers and exploitative winners may be a fantasy, but this can be a closer step to euphoria.

Extra Tip! Soccer has been the only sport to show any hint of progressivism in sports. If you insist your child play sports, put them in soccer.

TIPS FOR RAISING CHILDREN

Offensive Children Games

Hangman

Here is a game where kids actively partic-
ipate in the hanging of a black stick figure
man. Does more need to be said?

Spin the Bottle

The arbiter of consent is a bottle in this
game of chance. Our kids need to practice
real-world consensus of sexual activity,
rather than make a mockery of it.

Monopoly

For generations Monopoly has instilled
notions of greed and corruption to our
children. With no acts of redistribution and
incentive for capitalist power, this game
deserves to be trashed.

Laser Tag

There is something particularly disturbing
about children running around with guns
trying to "kill" as many other children as
possible.

TIPS FOR RAISING CHILDREN

#56 Associate with the Opposite.

There are traditional boy activities and traditional girl activities. But we can fuse these activities together and do away with vain traditions. Boys can be put into princess dresses and girls can play football. We can teach our children that gender is just a social construct by obligating them to do activities they may never do on their own.

TIPS FOR RAISING CHILDREN

#57 Mothers, Lock Your Sons Away!

Your sons are born sexual predators. It is in their nature to prey on women, particularly the weak and vulnerable. We need to believe all women when it comes to allegations of sexual misconduct and this certainly applies to the women that bring forward allegations against your sons. Do not give them the benefit of the doubt. If you do not want to be put in such a predicament, do not allow your sons a chance to be in a situation that could lead to an accusation. Keep them at home.

TIPS FOR RAISING CHILDREN

#58 Let them Vote.

Our children are left with the brutal task of fixing a future that has been destroyed by generations of incompetent adults. Kids have no choice but to sit idly by as we leave a shattered world for them to inherit. But that does not have to be the case. We can let them have a say. We can show real progress by giving our children a voice. Grab them from the monkey bars and put them in the voting booth. They are too young to see that R-rated movie, so give them a Bernie Sanders book to read. Remember, your children are under-educated, unemployed, irresponsible, and easily influenced, making them great Democratic voters.

TIPS FOR RAISING CHILDREN

#59 Explore Sexuality.

This may sound cringe-worthy, but only if you make it that way. Sexuality is a natural part of life and we can introduce our children to it at an early age as a way to make them more comfortable with it. Just take everyday activities and sprinkle in some perversion. For example, why have regular story time when you can have drag queen story time? This has already become a popular practice around the country. Or you can let your young, scantily dressed drag son dance in front of grown men as they throw money at him. We are at the point where this has already been accepted into society.

TIPS FOR RAISING CHILDREN

#60 Keep Them Publicly Educated.

Few avenues out there radicalize your children more than the public-school system. Do not lead their malleable minds astray by homeschooling or enrolling them in a private school. Teachers out there are fighting the good fight to ensure your children's indoctrination rolls perfectly into college. Do not deprive public school teachers and administrations their civic duty to enforce their beliefs onto your daughters and sons.

10 Tips for the College Campus

The college campus has become a haven of left-minded individuals. Use these tips to maximize on the opportunity to assimilate into the group-think of the University.

#61 Befriend a Professor

#62 Take Courses That Count

#63 Block the Hate

#64 Cite Marx

#65 Go Along to Get Along

#66 Diversity

#67 Administrative Reassurance

#68 Fight for Free

#69 Bring Back Segregation

#70 Use Your University in Your Introduction

TIPS FOR THE COLLEGE CAMPUS

#61 Befriend a Professor.

Throughout your college tenure, you are going to come across some of the brightest minds in academia. Take advantage of the accessibility you have and expand your knowledge outside of the classroom. Ask them how to vote. Ask them what to think of certain politicians. Ask them what their opinions are on controversial issues and mimic their exact talking points. Trust me, they will love nothing more than the opportunity to push their beliefs onto susceptible minds.

TIPS FOR THE COLLEGE CAMPUS

#62 Take Courses that Count.

Course Catalog

101 Radicalization
220 Racial Capitalism
300 Western Domination
350 Sexuality of Harry Potter
      and the Human Condition
400 Influence of the Phallus Form
600 Demystifying the Vagina

Taking courses that count does not necessarily apply to classes that directly attribute to your degree. Rather, they are courses that apply to life and the social fight that continues outside of the university. An undergraduate course catalog offers a bevy of hard-hitting and hyper aware classes that will help reinforce the indoctrination you are being put through.

TIPS FOR THE COLLEGE CAMPUS
#63 Block the Hate.

This is a politically challenging free campus

Detractors like to use the term "Free Speech" to invite what is truly considered hate speech on to the steps of our college campuses. Be on the lookout for the fringe student groups that look to challenge and upset the established order of academia. These groups like to bring in the most vile and putrid in the political sphere to regurgitate their filth in the form of speaking events. Write to administrators, to your professors, and demand that any upcoming event that promotes these haters be shut down immediately. No campus should be susceptible to challenging opinions.

TIPS FOR THE COLLEGE CAMPUS

#64 Cite Marx.

Want to appear as a bonafide college student? Keep these two guys in your back pocket. Karl Marx brought forward the true injustices between the economic classes and the repercussions of capitalist production. His writings in the "Communist Manifesto" paved the way for some of the major pillars of leftists today. Get a copy and make sure to study it. He is your god now.

TIPS FOR THE COLLEGE CAMPUS

#65 Go Along to Get Along.

Embrace the free following spirit of enlightenment on campus. Do not interfere with the almost militant agenda of the administrators, professors, and student organizations. Keep quiet in class and only speak up when your comments coincide with the professor or the collective. Universities are falling on dangerous times because we are allowing those in the minority think tank to mobilize and speak up on campus. Do not be mistaken for any of these deplorable students. Go along with the collective and you will get along with the university culture just fine.

TIPS FOR THE COLLEGE CAMPUS

#66 Diversity.

Diversity is great as long as you have a bunch of people that look different but think the same. Celebrate this beautiful diversity on your campus.

TIPS FOR THE COLLEGE CAMPUS

#67 Administrative Reassurance.

The administration is there when feelings are hurt. Any hurtful comment, disparaging look, upsetting election results, or just plain old-fashioned, unjustifiable complaining, you can always count on them to have your back. It may not help prepare you to work well with others in real life, but college is all about catering to your comfort.

TIPS FOR THE COLLEGE CAMPUS

#68 Fight for Free.

Education is not a privilege; it is a right, just like everything else we want others to pay for. Everyone deserves a chance at higher education, not just the wealthy few. We need younger generations to become institutionalized and that cannot happen with the continuing increase of costs for college. Tuition should be free in America and we need to continue to fight for that. College is about more than just building an educational path to a successful career. It is about opening your mind up and studying the unconventional. Where else can you study Lesbian Dance Theory at the tax payers' expense?

TIPS FOR THE COLLEGE CAMPUS

#69 Bring Back Segregation.

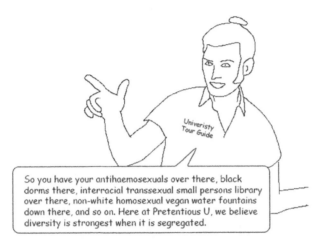

So you have your antihaemosexuals over there, black dorms there, interracial transsexual small persons library over there, non-white homosexual vegan water fountains down there, and so on. Here at Pretentious U, we believe diversity is strongest when it is segregated.

Do not be alarmed. This is not as racist as it sounds. By now, we have all heard of the term "Safe Spaces" on college campuses. These are imperative for students looking to retreat to an area that they know is impenetrable from outside forces that seek to harm their sensibility. Sometimes this includes spaces reserved for specific races, genders, sexualities, body types, cultures, or ideas. Your college campus should be comprised of multiple segregated groups that are safe and free practice self-expression. A collective and cohesive college campus in which students exchange thoughts openly among each other should just be labeled Hitler University.

TIPS FOR THE COLLEGE CAMPUS

#70 Use Your University in Your Introduction.

Actually, honey, my name is Alexander. Berkeley class of 1995. Nice to meet you.

This is my husband, Alex.

Now, not every university is worthy of a mention when you introduce yourself. If someone came up to you and said, "Hi, I am Bill, Columbia University class of 2004," wouldn't instant admiration for Bill shoot through your body like a liberal lightning bolt? Now imagine if Bill said Louisiana State University. Does not quite generate the same level of awe, does it? If you went to a prestigious university, you need to wear that the same way you wear your name. Let people know that you are refined and educated. They will respect you more for it.

10 Tips for the Work Place

Corporate culture has changed for the better. To keep progress going in the work place, you need to be vigilant on how you enforce your politics on co-workers. It is an every-day effort to force the company structure to comply to your ideologies. Fortunately, it doesn't take much to wake the office up to leftism!

#71 Display Your Heroes

#72 HR is an Ally

#73 "Would You Say That If"

#74 Never have Meetings with Women Alone

#75 Promote Company Wokeness

#76 Office Air Conditioning is Sexist

#77 Demand More

#78 Unionize

#79 Affirm

#80 Promote Equal Pay

TIPS FOR THE WORK PLACE

#71 Display Your Heroes.

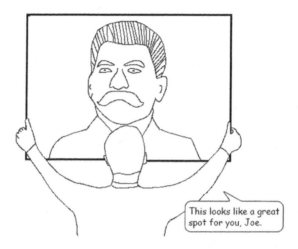

Politics is a bit of a taboo discussion around the office. However, there is a lingering desire to signal to everyone at the office that you belong to the party of rectitude. Here is a subtle way to shove that in the face of your coworkers. Hang picture, quotes, or portraits of some of the most prominent influencers of the left on your walls. Line your shelves with propaganda and books of progress. Also, remember that bumper stickers are not just for vehicles but make great wall decorations. Do this and your tolerant compassion will never be questioned.

TIPS FOR THE WORK PLACE

#72 HR is a Powerful Ally.

Human Resources is the police force of the workplace culture. With a single story or accusation, you could wipe out a career. HR has evolved throughout the years. Once believed to be the department of cover-up and corporate protection, it has now become the department of retribution. Do not get yourself on the wrong side of HR. Make no mistake; they are the most powerful division of any company.

TIPS FOR THE WORK PLACE

#73 "Would You Say That If..."

Here is one of those great tips that will get you out of any situation, but only contingent on if you meet the criteria. You might find yourself in trouble at work, whether it is coming in late, taking too many days off, missing a deadline, or slacking behind an over-achieving co-worker. Being a white male prevents you from using this line unless you are homosexual, which even then still vaguely applies. Next time you find yourself in a sticky situation or on the brink of being terminated, throw this in your boss's face and watch them squirm. They will never mess with you again.

TIPS FOR THE WORK PLACE

#74 Never have Meetings with Women Alone.

Thanks, Donna, for meeting with me for dinner. You have been a valuable client to the firm. Oh, and this is my female attorney, Barbara. She is just here to advise on everything I should and shouldn't say.

As a man, you are bound to say something misogynistic. It's inevitable that something offensive will come out of your mouth, even if it is the littlest invasive comment such as asking how the kids are doing. If you want to avoid a trip to HR, take this tip seriously. Do not even think of traveling alone with a woman, calling a woman into a closed-door meeting in your office, having a work dinner or lunch or, heaven forbid, having a drink with a woman co-worker or client. This is known as the Pence rule after the bigoted Vice-President Mike Pence, who will not meet with women unless his wife is present. Unfortunately, it turns out he was right about one thing.

TIPS FOR THE WORK PLACE

#75 Promote Company Wokeness.

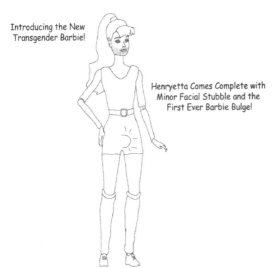

Introducing the New Transgender Barbie!

Henryetta Comes Complete with Minor Facial Stubble and the First Ever Barbie Bulge!

Your company needs to be on the cutting edge of every political opportunity that is presented. The first reason your company needs to be "woke" is because it is profitable and, let's be honest, this is the most important reason of all. Chances are your company will sell more units if it shows it supports Gay Pride Month. It will build more brand loyalty if the company advertises in a way that disparages anyone to the right of you. We have already seen this from large corporations such as Nike, Gillette, and Target. They have set the bar for how a good corporation should act and there is no reason you cannot bring that attitude to your company. Then you can feel good about working for a company with such high morals—even if the morals are only centered on making a profit.

TIPS FOR THE WORK PLACE

#76 Office Air Conditioning is Sexist.

There is an AC war taking place in your office, and menfolk are winning. You don't need scientific studies to realize that the office temperature is blatantly set to a man's comfort. They pay no mind to the women with blankets thrown over their shivering bodies, desk heaters desperately warming their legs, or frail, stiff fingers pecking away at keyboards in frozen anguish. As long as the patriarch is warm on his perch, no one else matters. If you are a man, help flip this narrative by cranking up the thermostat a few degrees. If you sweat profusely, simply shed off articles of clothing to a point where it doesn't become sexual harassment. Despite your sweltering misery, at least you help bring a bit of progress to the office.

TIPS FOR THE WORK PLACE

#77 Demand More.

Living wages are still out of reach for many Americans. Instead, they are living with a never-ending death wage—a wage so low that it makes it nearly impossible to live a flourishing lifestyle. If you are trapped in the inhumane grips of a minimum wage at your current occupation, you need to petition for more. It doesn't matter if your demand to increase your wage puts a small business out of business. It doesn't matter if you don't produce any additional output or add any value to justify an increase in wage. It doesn't matter if your hours get cut and you end up making less with a higher wage. All that matters is that you are entitled to more and you will do whatever it takes to get there.

TIPS FOR THE WORK PLACE

Office Do's; Office Don'ts

DO NOT

Ask female employees how the kids are doing. This implies that, since they are women, the only thing you can discuss is kids.

DO NOT

Put Fox News on any of the TVs in the break area. Make sure those areas are safe spaces for you and fellow employees.

DO NOT

Limit one's ability to freely express themselves by implementing a dress code.

DO NOT

Celebrate any particular holiday in the office, especially if you have to say Merry Christmas. You never know who you will offend.

DO

Ask them if they caught the game last night. Ask about if they have seen that great action-packed flick you saw. Treat them like you would treat another man.

DO

Put on something safe and comforting that will put the office at ease through an otherwise chaotic day at the office. Something like CNN.

DO

Let employees wear whatever they want, expose any kind of piercing, tattoo or political statement piece.

DO

Keep holidays neutral around the office. Keep your office and desk free of any decorations that some may find threatening, like a Christmas tree.

TIPS FOR THE WORK PLACE

#78 Unionize.

The current right-to-work laws have eradicated the ability to force co-workers into paying in union dues or face termination. This has seriously impeded the unions' ability to force employees to fund candidates and positions they do not support. But that doesn't mean you still can't rally the troops and form up against the exploitation of workers. After all, no one reaps more benefits from exploitation of workers than the head of the union.

TIPS FOR THE WORK PLACE

#79 Affirm.

There is no better qualification for a job than being part of a minority group. It doesn't matter if your credentials are nowhere near the next deserving candidate. Keep this in mind when you are applying, not just for a job but for anything. Even the slightest minority ancestry can guarantee a spot at another person's expense.

TIPS FOR THE WORK PLACE

#80 Promote Equal Pay.

I don't get it, Johnny! We fired all the men in the company and hired women. I thought you said they make less than men? Why are we not seeing significant cost cuts?

A common fallacy the patriarch likes to proclaim in defense of the wage gap is that woman make different career choices and opt for lower-paying jobs. Like societal pressure gives women a choice. Men, and unfortunately some women, too, are constantly adding variables to an equation that still adds up to women being paid less. Some of these trivial variables include more men in college pursuing STEM degrees while women tend to go into humanitarian studies. Or for doctors, where men tend to go into specialties such as neurosurgery, while women go into lower-paying areas such as pediatrics. But a doctor is a doctor. A woman pediatrician should make as much as a male brain surgeon, just like a WNBA basketball player should make as much as an NBA player. They are both professional basketball players so there is no rationality for a pay gap. Throw out all the other variables and focus on a singular number that not only shows women are paid less but also proves all jobs are sexist.

10 Tips for Marriage/Dating

The social stigma of being in a monotonous relationship plagues us all if we let it. If you opt into this construct, here are a few tips to follow to make sure that at least you are happy in the relationship.

#81 Last Name Claim

#82 Date Only Your Color

#83 Date Screening

#84 Leave 'Em

#85 Pay for the Date

#86 Stay Childless

#87 Date for Fun, Not Marriage

#88 You Do Not Need Religion

#89 Polygamy is Key

#90 You Do Not Need Anyone

TIPS FOR MARRIAGE/DATING

#81 Last Name Claim.

There is no written rule (except in perhaps the book of patriarchal control) that states someone is obligated to take a man's last name in marriage. A woman should keep her name. She has a credible claim to keep her lineage alive just as much as any man does. If you and your spouse cannot agree, at the very least, hyphenate the two names. However, this may get a little wordy if both of your last names are already hyphenated. Better yet, start a new line of progressive lineage and both you and your spouse can conjure up a new name together!

TIPS FOR MARRIAGE/DATING

#82 Date Your Color.

Interracial couples are all well and fine but there comes a point where the preservation of race needs considerable contemplation. And I am only speaking of preserving minority races. Comfort and understanding will always lie within your same race, especially when you live in one of the most racially divisive times of our history. Help heal the constant anguish in this country by limiting yourself to a same-race dating pool.

TIPS FOR MARRIAGE/DATING

#83 Date Screen.

During a date, it is always important to get to know the person through a series of typical questions, such as what do you do for a living, where are you from, do you have any siblings, blah, blah, blah. Let's cut to the chase and ask the hard-hitting questions that will determine if the date will even continue for another five seconds, depending on the answer. Who did you vote for? Are you a Democrat? Leave them with the check and a scolding mix of insults and animosity if they respond with anything to the right of Alinsky.

TIPS FOR MARRIAGE/DATING

#84 Leave 'Em.

Horror stories of adultery were abundant in 2016. I'm not talking about spouses hiding intimate relationships with others. I'm talking about unfaithfulness of ideology. I'm talking about the cheating of the mind and principles, which is by far a more unforgiveable betrayal. Spouses that break the very foundation that your marriage was built upon have tainted a level of trust that can never be redeemed. This is not a matter of mere political disagreement, but insanity versus sane. You cannot make a commitment to someone that supports the destruction of morality and compassion. Save yourself the misery of forced reconciliation and use any means necessary to get out.

TIPS FOR MARRIAGE/DATING

#85 Pay for the Date.

Outdated masculinity rules say the guy should always pay for the first date and beyond. A typical male will always turn this around on a female as if she is now indebted to him for providing the financial resources to ingest food. Next thing you know, you'll be staying at home with no career and your only purpose in life will be to bear his children. In the same sense, a woman's cost to prepare for a date is much higher than a man's. With makeup, clothes and other beauty products, not to mention the emotional stress of how to look, there is never an equal playing field for a date. A man should never presume to cover the cost of a date nor should he let a woman feel the burden of the additional expense.

TIPS FOR MARRIAGE/DATING

#86 Stay Childless.

We have enough people in the world ruining our ecosystem by scourging the earth of natural resources. The selfish act of bringing a child into this world only brings our planet one more step closer to annihilation. Instead, focus efforts on your marriage as well as yourself. Caring and raising another human being only restricts you from being your best self. Do the world and yourself a favor and skip the kids. If for some reason you absolutely feel the need to care for something other than yourself, there are plenty of animals that need homes. This is a great substitute that allows you to claim parenthood without introducing the little carbon footprint.

Extra Tip! Do not adopt. This only strengthens the argument for pro-life nut jobs.

TIPS FOR MARRIAGE/DATING

#87 Date for Fun, not Marriage.

An outstanding tip to marriage is simply do not get married. Much like children, marriage requires your time and effort to care for someone other than yourself. You have your activism, your morals, and your free spirit ambitions to concentrate on. It may be an unfulfilling void, but that is the price of being relationship-free. Date for the sex, for the free meals, and for the social gatherings that make a pretend monogamous relationship acceptable.

TIPS FOR MARRIAGE/DATING

Great Excuses for No Kids and No Marriage

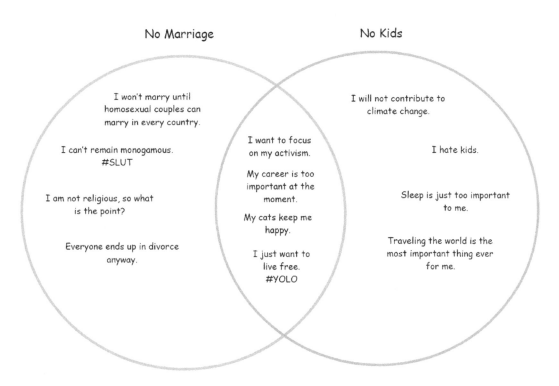

No Marriage

No Kids

I won't marry until homosexual couples can marry in every country.

I can't remain monogamous. #SLUT

I am not religious, so what is the point?

Everyone ends up in divorce anyway.

I want to focus on my activism.

My career is too important at the moment.

My cats keep me happy.

I just want to live free. #YOLO

I will not contribute to climate change.

I hate kids.

Sleep is just too important to me.

Traveling the world is the most important thing ever for me.

TIPS FOR MARRIAGE/DATING

#88 You Do Not Need Religion.

Forgo a foundation of religion in the relationship. This is just added pressure to abide by fictitious rules that turn a relationship into a jail sentence. Make marriage what you want it to be and how you define the role each partner takes. No sacred text is going to guarantee happiness in what is already an outdated practice. Only you and your partner have that responsibility. Use political principles as a guide to a healthy relationship of shared values and morals. Praise politicians like they are your gods to fill that empty pit in your soul that wrongfully calls for religion.

TIPS FOR MARRIAGE/DATING

#89 Polygamy is Key.

If your partner is not open to a polygamous relationship, do they really love you? If you love something, you set if free, even if by setting them "free" means being okay with your partner banging it out with a total stranger behind a Denny's. We are progressing past the traditional single partner-type marriages and relationships. I get that not everyone is on board with this but your partner may feel different and want to explore his or her options, knowing he or she always has you to fall back on. Always keep an open mind, not just in politics, but in the bedroom, too.

TIPS FOR MARRIAGE/DATING

#90 You Do Not Need Anyone.

Truth is, you have your activism, liberalism, and self-gratification that no other human can provide. Buckling under social pressure is one of the many reasons relationships fail. You don't need it. Stay single and maintain your independence. You belong to belong to no one, nor do you owe anything to anyone. It's bitter. It's lonely. But it's empowering!

10 Tips for the Internet and Social Media

All activism requires a social media presence. #WOKE

#91 Doxing

#92 Uncovering

#93 Keep Talk Tough

#94 Random Rants

#95 Spread it

#96 Report Posts

#97 Celebrity-Follow

#98 Bully

#99 Plead for Donations

#100 Pretend Happiness

TIPS FOR THE INTERNET AND SOCIAL MEDIA

#91 Doxing.

Antifa Front ∨

@antifa

We will be tweeting out the addresses of all pundits
that labeled us a domestic terror group. Don't worry;
@Twitter will not do anything about it.
GO DO YOUR WORST.

3/1/2020, 8:00am

You may be wondering, what exactly is doxing? Well, it is a powerful tool against your adversaries and has been practiced by countless people, including those in the media. When you dox someone, you are publicly releasing a person's information online without their consent. This includes their phone number, home address, place of work, wife/husband's place of work, kids' school, etc. Once you have doxed them, you can gather the mob and implement tip #27. Send a message of fear to the next person that dares to cross you.

#92 Uncovering.

Uncovering is a worthwhile tactic, especially when paired with doxing. Take time to go back on a target's social media to find any and all posts that can paint this person as some kind of monster. Remember that social media is a great place to start if you need to assassinate someone's character, as stated in rule #15. Any little thing will do, even if it is taken out of context. Use what you find to define that person as a whole. Yes, people change, but perception is important. A single tweet can define a person's career. A picture can ruin a person's life. A post can negate everything positive a person has done. It's out there; you just need to find it.

TIPS FOR THE INTERNET AND SOCIAL MEDIA

#93 Keep Talk Tough.

Let's do battle.

You can be whatever you desire on the internet. Whether it is a Che Guevara-type revolutionary or a Friedrich Engels-esque philosopher, no one will know your true self. Take this attitude to the comments section of any article and do yeoman's work. Hurl insults and empty threats to establish internet dominance and take pride in doing so. On the web, you can be the king of clout, the duke of trumptard destruction, the intellectual menace. What is even better is that you can do it all from the comfort of your parents' basement.

TIPS FOR THE INTERNET AND SOCIAL MEDIA

#94 Spread It.

Before a story gets debunked or people actually read the article instead of just the headline, be sure to help spread that information. The media is on our side and we need to help them in return by making sure misleading and fake news creates the narrative we all want. Sharing is caring. Show you actually care by giving the people a chance to form a false perspective before any headline is debunked.

TIPS FOR THE INTERNET AND SOCIAL MEDIA

#95 Do Random Rants.

Injustice is met with complacency each and every day in this abhorrent nation. You have a virtual voice, so use it to rant! Post 5-10 times daily to make sure you flood your followers' news feeds with excessive whining. Speak truth to power and become the arbiter of social media social justice. Stir up controversy by ranting on someone else's post and divert attention to yourself. We all know we love the attention. This is how we spread our emotion-driven politics, by constantly inundating people with our streams of consciousness.

TIPS FOR THE INTERNET AND SOCIAL MEDIA

#96 Report Posts.

Social media companies do a prestigious job of censoring conservative content on their own. However, this does not mean a few things tend to slip through the cracks. They need you to be their outsourced watchdog to make sure those platforms are cleansed of deplorable rhetoric. Any post can be flagged, whether it is egregious or just minorly offensive. Share the duty of policing all ideas on social media and limit posting abilities of those you'd rather never hear from.

TIPS FOR THE INTERNET AND SOCIAL MEDIA

#97 Celebrity-Follow.

As stated back in tip #14, our objectives are eternally culturally backed. If you have no opinion, find an opinion. Follow the numerous celebrities that repeat the same talking points among themselves in an infinite Hollywood echo chamber. They are authoritative figures on politics and conjure up tirades that can simply be repeated during conversations. No reason to try to come up with your own thoughts!

TIPS FOR THE INTERNET AND SOCIAL MEDIA

Who to Follow? Start with the Talk Show Hosts.

Oh, boy, do we have the monopoly over late night talk show TV. They make great little puppets for executives at these media conglomerates. What they say may not be brave. It may be a bit conforming. They might be repetitive and unoriginal. But these talk show hosts are a great start to celebrity social media following. No one actually stays up to watch these shows unless they are under the age of 22. Catch clips of each episode on social media and watch as these shows disguise their narrative-pushing agendas as mediocre comedy. You will be well informed as well as mildly entertained.

Bill Maher

Stephen Colbert

Samantha Bee

John Oliver

Jimmy Kimmel

Trevor Noah

TIPS FOR THE INTERNET AND SOCIAL MEDIA

#98 Bully.

Ivana Attention
October 30 at 7:39 PM · 🌐   •••

Why does Ben Shapiro even have an outlet to spread lies? Are we supposed to believe the things that short Jewish guys say now?

👍 Like   💬 Comment   ↗ Share

Bullying is not a typical behavior we condone but, like with many things, this is a "do as we say, not as we do" type of issue. That being said, bullying is something you do want to do. Knock down those fascists a peg or two. Point to flaws in physical attributes or mock their religious beliefs, and do not forget their families are susceptible to scrutiny as well. If you are worried about backlash, your bullying will blend in with the rest of the comments on social media so there will be no individual targeting of you.

TIPS FOR THE INTERNET AND SOCIAL MEDIA

#99 Plead for Donations.

Miss Misérable
September 1 at 3:09 PM · 🌐

•••

Please donate to my GoFundMe so I can donate to Planned Parenthood.

👍 Like   💬 Comment   ↪ Share

Let's be honest, liberals are not known for their generous donations. That doesn't mean that we can ask others to pick up our slack. We are more compassionate in the verbal sense than we are the substantive kind. Take the verbal compassion to your social media posts and dictate to others that they need to take financial action. You will be recognized for your passionate post, relieving you of any obligation to contribute monetary value.

TIPS FOR THE INTERNET AND SOCIAL MEDIA

#100 Pretend Happiness.

Being angry and triggered on a constant basis can really make you a miserable person. Keep your virtual head up. Fake a smile for a selfie and let your followers know that you are a content social justice warrior, not the self-loathing, bitter person you truly are.

CONCLUSION

#101 Do Not Follow These Tips.

Satire is often lost on people of both the right and left. This is why, for the second time, I will state unequivocally that these tips are 100% satire! Now, if these tips are mistaken to be something of actual applicable value, I would suggest you watch something other than CNN, reading something other than the Huffington Post, and finding a healthy hobby. Yet, it is not so far-fetched that these could be mistaken for a sort of ultra-progressive check list compiled by Don Lemon, Bill Ayers, and Alexandria Ocasio-Cortez. After all, these tips were inspired by true events that take place in the circus tent that has become our daily news cycle. There is a level of outrageous exaggeration in satire. The difference is that, while these tips might be outrageous, they are not completely exaggerated, given that many are practiced every day.

Sincerely, Tanner T. Roberts

5 Tips for Conservatives

I would be remiss if I excluded a list of tips for conservatives to follow. The fact is, hypocrisy in politics is not a one-party issue. While the tips for going from liberal to left have been nothing but a complete parody, the tips for conservatives serve better as a hard truth.

#1 Boycotting

#2 Blind Support

#3 Not My President

#4 Pretending Culture Doesn't Matter

#5 Whataboutism

TIPS FOR CONSERVATIVES

#1 Boycotting.

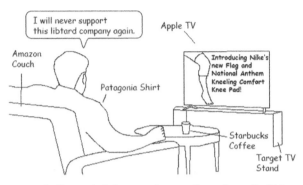

One of the many glories of capitalism is the ability for consumers to make choices amid competing products. Whether you decide to purchase based on price, functionality, or any other metrics, the decision is strictly yours. However, many consumers use a singular metric that is more influential than price or function. Politics weighs more on consumer decisions as many corporations rush to virtue profit signaling. What many conservatives fail to do is see the hypocrisy in these kinds of decisions. They will not step foot in a Target but will buy Amazon stock. They will get on their iPhones to leave a comment on a post on Facebook about how liberal Costco is from their research on Google. We cannot cherry-pick certain companies with opposing leadership ideologies while continuing to support others for consumption convenience. If your consumer behavior is based on a guiding set of principles and values, those values should apply equally. Otherwise, you are buying based on outrage rather than any sense of fabricated morals. In the end, it is employees that suffer, and some of the employees do not hold the same ideals as the company that employees them.

TIPS FOR CONSERVATIVES

#2 Blind Support

Too often, conservatives give politicians the benefit of the doubt simply because there is an "R" at the end of their name. I'm here to tell you that it is not only okay to criticize your own party, but it's American. The leaders of this country need to be kept in check, especially those from your own party, and you cannot do that by justifying every action or comment that is contradictory to your values.

Quit making martyrs out of government employees and come to realize they are not flawless human beings. There is no one you should ever agree with 100%, especially anyone in politics. Blind support like this is borderline fanatic. What is even more lunatic is how devotees tend to back their politicians by name-calling critics of the same party. They are liberals because they do not agree with a trade policy. They are leftist because they condemn useless comments. They are hippies because they do not support a military operation. Just stop the mindless advocacy and realize that support is conditional, not definitive, in politics.

TIPS FOR CONSERVATIVES

#3 Not My President

Just because you did not vote for the current president does not make it a disputable fact that he or she is not your president. No matter how big a tantrum you throw, the validity of the Oval Office is not dictated by your approval. The height of this ignorance was seen in the 2008 election of Barack Obama where "Not My President" became a tagline for those that opposed our 44th president. This was emulated to unprecedented extremes in 2016 after the election of Trump. I urge conservatives not to engage in this embarrassing behavior that essentially pits them against reality.

TIPS FOR CONSERVATIVES

#4 Pretending Culture Doesn't Matter.

Conservatives have been losing the culture battle for decades and have remained completely complacent in that fact. In media, Hollywood and education is the axis that has become so tilted that many have written it off as a useless battle. A singular narrative is constantly pushed and we are to believe this isn't a fight worth pursuing. As Andrew Breitbart once famously said, "Politics is downstream from culture." Media is not just about news and entertainment. It promotes ideas, feelings, moods, and attitudes. Media tells us what is important and controls that narrative. Sitting idly by as these outlets are taken over just isn't going to do it anymore.

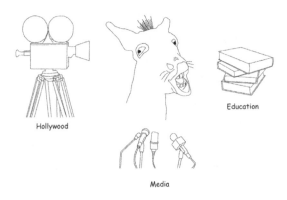

Hollywood

Education

Media

#5 Whataboutism

You have to admit that was a pretty dumb thing for Trump to say.

The What About Buttons

Bill Clinton AOC Barack Obama Nancy Pelosi

Illhan Ohmar Bernie Sander Hillary Clinton Anthony Wiener

Hold on.

Deflection is an essential strategic maneuver when you blindly support members in politics. Typically, that deflection involves engagement of "Whataboutism." Whataboutism is the simple act redirecting the wrongdoing of one individual by asking "What about" the actions of another individual who has committed equal or greater offenses. People try to use whataboutism as an excuse or justification of someone else's behavior. Conservatives tend to become too eager to call out hypocrisy when given the opportunity to point the finger. Two things are allowed to be true at once: You can denounce the actions of you someone you support and you can call out the hypocrisy of liberals when they do not hold the same moral standards for their leaders. So, when Donald Trump tweets that certain American-born congresswomen should go back to where they come from as he did in July 2019, it is okay to condemn those words. After all, it is un-American to tell those who politically disagree with you to leave the country. It is not okay to immediately point out the numerous foul things those congresswomen have said as if to say one action is justified by the other. Condemn and then call out hypocrisy. Remember this next time you ask, "Well, what about Hillary Clinton or what about Barack Obama?"

Made in the USA
Monee, IL
19 December 2020